Moving House

Rebecca Hunter

Photography by Chris Fairclough

Evans

PET

First Times
My First Day at School
My First School Play
My New Sister
My First Visit to Hospital
My New Dad
Moving House
My First Pet
My First Visit to London

Published by Evans Brothers Ltd
2A Portman Mansions
Chiltern Street
London W1M 1LE
England

First published in 2000

British Library Cataloguing in Publication Data
Hunter, Rebecca
Moving House. - (First Times)
1. Moving, Household - Juvenile literature
I. Title
648.9

ISBN 0 237 52019 2

Acknowledgements
Planning and production by Discovery Books
Editor: Rebecca Hunter
Photographer: Chris Fairclough
Designer: Ian Winton
Consultant: Trevor Jellis M.A., M.Phil., A.F.B.Ps., Psychol. is a Chartered Psychologist who has spent thirty years working with individuals, schools, companies and major corporate institutions in the management of stress. He deals with individuals who are suffering from stress both in their family and in the workplace.

The publishers would like to thank Stephanie Bloomfield, Linda and Jeremy Bloomfield, Anthony Burgess and Arabella Midwood for their help in the preparation of this book.

Contents

My house is for sale.

My house is for sale. We are going to move house.

6

I don't want to move.

Mum and Dad
show me pictures
of the new house.
The new house
looks nice but I
still don't want
to move.

I will miss our road.

I will miss playing
with the children in
our road. I will also miss
my friends at school.

I will miss my garden.

I will miss my garden and my swing. I wonder if the new garden will have a tree for a swing.

It is time to pack up.

It is time to pack up. I help Mum and Dad. We have to wrap things in newspaper so they won't break.

I pack my toys.

I am in my playroom packing my toys. I have a lot of toys so I will need lots of boxes.

The removal men arrive.

The removal men arrive in their big lorry.

They are going to move our furniture to the new house.

MISTER MOVER

They let me help.

They carry all our things into the lorry. They let me help. It takes all morning to empty our house.

Our new house is bigger.

This is our new house. It is bigger than our old house. The garden is bigger too.

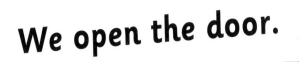

We open the door.

Dad gets out the key.
It is exciting opening the
door for the first time.

The men unload all our things.

The removal men have to unload all our things.

It is tiring work, they are glad to have a cup of tea.

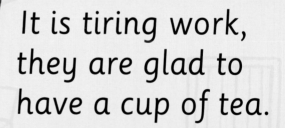

Now we have to unpack.

Our new house is full of boxes.

Mum and I unpack the boxes of kitchen things first.

We are painting my bedroom.

We have lived here for two weeks now.

Mum and I are painting animals and birds on the walls in my new bedroom.

I have a new friend.

I have a new friend called Bella. She lives next door. She has a playhouse. We are playing at moving house!

I am glad we moved house.

Index

Notes to Parents and Teachers

Moving house is a big event for a small child. Children like familiar places and routines. The old house will hold precious memories and be regarded as safe. Friendships will have developed in the neighbourhood through nursery and play. The garden will be a special place full of memories. Leaving the old house may be their first experience of loss and a small child will be uncertain as to what lies ahead.

Parents can begin to prepare the child when the old house first goes on the market. They need to emphasise all the positive things about having a new house – having a different bedroom, an exciting new garden, new friends, a new school etc. When the child expresses concern or unhappiness, it is important that parents talk through the situation with the child. It may take some time for the child to settle in the new area. Talking through the child's anxieties is very important and should not be rushed.

• To move successfully requires a lot of planning and preparation for adults. The same care should be taken in preparing children.

• The new house can be visited before the move and the parents can discuss with the child which room she would like as a bedroom/ playroom etc.

• Parents can arrange for the child to meet any children in the new area before they move.

• Teachers should be aware that children may seem insecure before they move house, and after the event will take some time to settle down in their new school.